Skindulgence
Urban Retreat Ltd.
Port Moody, B.C.
604 469 2688

Fifty Ways
to Feed
Your
Soul

Fifty Ways
to Feed
Your
Soul

ROSEMARY CUNNINGHAM

A *Spirituality & Health* Book

Red Wheel
Boston, MA / York Beach, ME

First published in 2004 by Red Wheel/Weiser, LLC
York Beach, ME
With offices at:
368 Congress Street, Boston, MA 02210
www.redwheelweiser.com

Library of Congress Cataloging-in-Publication Data
Fifty ways to feed your soul / [edited by] Rosemary Cunningham.
    p. cm.
  "A spirituality & health book."
  ISBN 1-59003-069-9 (alk. paper)
 1. Spiritual life. I. Cunningham, Rosemary,
  BL624.F499 2004
  204'.32--dc22

                   2004000288

Typeset in MrsEavesRoman by Jill Feron/Feron Design

Printed in Canada
Friesens
11 10 09 08 07 06 05 04
 8 7 6 5 4 3 2 1

The paper used in this publication meets the minimum requirements
of the American National Standard for Information Sciences—Permanence
of Paper for Printed Library Materials Z39.48-1992 (R1997).

This book is dedicated to my parents:
Thomas P. Cunningham
Jane Davey Cunningham Graffam
Dr. Donald T. Graffam
Gone so long. Lovingly remembered.

Contents

Acknowledgments

At the heart of this book are forty-nine people I have never met but whose spirited sharing has been a vital part of my world since shortly after September 11, 2001. Acting as the shepherd for their nourishing words has played an important part in my healing from that time of intense grief and fear. It was an unexpected gift that I continue to treasure.

This book was coaxed into life by generosity of spirit. It is the direct result of the support, faith, and encouragement of these people:

Mary Ann Brussat	Stephen Kiesling
Frederic A. Brussat	Dinie Lowenstein
Julia Cameron	Lilan Patri
Rochelle Friedlich	Robert Owens Scott
Fran Greenfield	Carrie Thompson
Pat Hartley	Wondrous *Artist Way* friends

Above all, this is God's book.
Thank You, Great Who, for the opportunity.

Introduction

We're all connected. The thread may be invisible but it is there. And it is here in this book. What connects us is our seeking. We may travel different paths and they may lead us to different answers, but it is in our seeking that we are the same.

Almost a decade ago I realized I hungered for more God. I believed in a loving presence larger than myself, but that presence seemed to be available only in certain places or at certain times. Sometimes I didn't even remember there was a God, I was so consumed by the people, places, and things around me. Slowly it dawned on me that I was loved and connected, but maybe I just wasn't paying attention. And so it began. I started to create ways to open myself to the presence of a living, loving God in each moment of my day. I didn't have a name for it then, but today I realize I had begun to practice feeding my soul.

Instead of using my imagination to frighten myself about the future or to attempt to rewrite the past, I put it to use thinking up ways to remember that God is always in the present. Each morning I selected and copied a brief spiritual quote on a 3" x 5" card to carry in my pocket all day. Now I carry a little rosewood box with the word "Faith" carved in its top. Inside are three pieces of silver with these words engraved on them: "Patience," "Trust," and "Courage." When I reach into my pocket I may not remember the exact words, but I am reminded of God.

I also began to use my Walkman to listen to tapes I made for myself. I chose songs that focused on faith and God's love. I shifted my focus to understand many traditional love songs as love-from-God songs. For instance, I made a tape of "How Deep Is the Ocean?" recorded repeatedly on both sides. I used it to try and get an inkling of how much God loves us all.

I re-envisioned everyday places and activities. I began thinking of bathrooms as prayer stalls and elevators as meditation booths. Waiting in line became an opportunity to connect with God. A trip to the grocery store became the chance to silently bless everyone I saw.

Several years ago I began walking to a nearby river. At first I resented the river because it wasn't the ocean! But I felt drawn there, so I kept going anyway. I did nothing more than stand in the same place every day and watch. I paid attention to the river, and in time, she revealed the presence of God in her profound, ever-changing beauty.

Recently, inspired by Tibetan prayer flags, I used green yarn, gold tissue paper, rainbow-colored ribbons, photos, and words to create my own prayer flags. The breeze through my home ruffles the hanging flags, spreading these prayers of gratitude for just 34 of the people, places, and things of wonder I encountered in one week of my life. Gradually these practices and others have transformed a formerly invisible God into a God whose presence is increasingly visible in my day.

Along the way, I sought out other seekers as I participated in established spiritual practices that interested me, such as the labyrinth, Quaker meetings, Friday night Shabbat services, a variety of Christian worship services, Sufi Zikr, Taizé Prayer, new moon circles, and

Jewish healing services. Each practice and each person I encountered enriched my relationship with God. Some of them became an integral part of my life. Over time I relaxed and began to savor the journey as I looked not for the right practices but for practices that were right for me.

Several weeks after September 11, I got a call from Bob Scott, editor of *Spirituality & Health.* The magazine planned to gather submissions from its readers to create a piece on ways to nourish your soul, and Bob wondered if I would be interested in working on the project. As we talked, I told Bob about a friend who had just called to report the happy results of a much-feared mammogram. My friend celebrated by painting the words "healthy" and "beautiful" on her breasts for her own viewing and delight. Her playful, poetic action set us to thinking about the many ways we each feed our souls—frequently without realizing that's what we are doing.

We invited the magazine's readers to reflect on their daily lives and to share the simple actions that nourished their souls. We asked, "How do you feed your soul? Have you done something spontaneous on a particular occasion? Or do you have a daily ritual that deepens your connection to your essential self, to the world, and to God?" Responses came via e-mail from around the country and the world. Many of them became a magazine article and now are the heart of this book.

Our hope is that the practices in this book provide you with new perspective on the moments of your own life. Perhaps simply reading them will do that or maybe you'll incorporate one or more of these practices into your life. Something you read here might help you identify an activity you participate in now, or did at one time, as being soul nurturing. Or you might be inspired to create your own ways to feed your soul.

I once read that a beloved spiritual teacher asked his students, "Where is God?" A bright-eyed student answered eagerly, "God is everywhere." "No," said the teacher. "God is where we let Him in." This book is about just that: people like you and me letting God in.

How This Book Is Organized

Over the past year I have been blessed with the opportunity to feed my soul by following many of the suggestions in this book. I found, just as their authors did, that they transformed my experiences of the people, places, and things in my life. So I've grouped them that way: by People, Places, and Things. You'll find that interactions with animals appear in the "People" section. If you've ever had an animal companion, you'll know why.

People

If I know what love is, it is because of you.
—HERMAN HESSE

There is nothing new in this book. But there is something very powerful here: the power of *we*. These ways of connecting with the Holy One don't require fancy equipment, fancy clothes, or even fancy spiritual maneuvers. They do require the humility to acknowledge that we need—and can learn from—one another.

Everything I know about a loving God I learned from someone else. Whether I read it, overheard it, or spied it in action, it was wisdom passed on to me. As the African proverb says, "You don't need to be tall to see the moon." Just stand where you are. Sooner or later the moon will appear. Sooner or later I'll see the God in you.

1

Catch the Enthusiasm

I nourish my soul by watching my three-year-old daughter eat. When something she's eating is delicious, my heart actually quivers. Her enthusiasm for life and sustenance is contagious.

—VIVA DELGADO, California

Connect

Whenever I feel the need to remember that I am a child of God, I call friends or acquaintances and ask how they are. This simple act reminds me that a word or deed—however inconsequential—sends the powerful message that God is all love, and each time we share that love with another person with a word or smile, we create a powerful force in the world that combats fear and loneliness.

—ELIZABETH SIMONS, Missouri

3

Go on a Playdate

A good friend and I make time once or twice a month for a girls' night out. It's never anything elaborate, perhaps some shopping or an evening class (we took line dancing together last spring) and dinner at an inexpensive restaurant. Just a few hours to connect with one another, away from our family obligations, makes a world of difference!

—LISA RUBIN, New York

4

Harmonize

Children's music and Christmas music always feed my soul and take me to a place of gentle innocence and happiness. On stressful days and in rush-hour traffic, I give my soul flight when I tune in to my favorite songs. Sometimes the children and I sing along and it always makes us smile and act silly.

—LeAnn Malecha, Illinois

5

Actively Love Yourself

When I awaken every morning I look in the mirror before washing my face. Tenderly looking into my own eyes, I cross my hands over my heart and say to the familiar face, "How can I remember to be more loving, juicy, and joyful with you today?" It sets the intention for the hours ahead and keeps me focused on what is truly important.

—SYLVIA COHEN, New York

7

6

Be Kind

Although I hadn't thought of it in this way before, I suppose what nourishes my soul the most is when a situation arises where I can spontaneously offer help or an anonymous kindness. It may be as simple as gathering a few stray shopping carts from the parking lot and putting them in their place. Often it's visiting with strangers—usually senior citizens—who cross my path on any given day and really enjoy having someone to visit with for a few minutes.

—SHERI McCALL, Missouri

Appreciate Loved Ones

Whenever I hear my daughter sing or my son laugh, I stop and thank God for my children, their safety, and God's guidance to me and their father for raising them. I remember that soon I'll be looking back on these days, perhaps with longing, and that I must treat my children as dear guests who are about to leave.

—ELLEN M. COSGROVE, Maryland

Take a Dog's-Eye View

I make pet visits to the local hospital with my golden retriever, Dakota. My schedule has us visiting oncology patients and their families. Dakota's schedule has us visiting everyone. We greet all the housekeeping staff, the people outside the hospital in the smoking area, the office staff, hospital volunteers, and anyone else he sees. When I'm with Dakota, I *see* and talk to many more people than when I'm alone. It's my goal in life to *see* everyone—as he does—even when he's not with me.

–SUSAN H. SKINNER, Iowa

Sit Quietly in a Room Alone

Whenever I feel down and out, I shut myself in a room and sit quietly and meditate. I think of all I have to be grateful for. Sometimes I think about something charming or funny my kids have said recently so that I smile, and sometimes I just close my eyes, breathe deeply, and let myself be.

—ABHA IYENGAR, India

10

Take Care of Your Precious Self

After my father died of colon cancer, I knew I needed to have a colonoscopy and be screened for colon cancer. It wasn't something I looked forward to. But when I thought of it as an act of self-nurture, I dreaded it less. It truly was an act of self-nurture because knowing that I'm cancer free gives me a sense of relief every time I think of it.

—DIANE DORA, Iowa

11

Allow Others to Pray for You

Chemotherapy has given me an unexpected gift. I find that I must go within and connect with my soul on a daily basis. It has brought me closer to myself. I am more aware of the rhythms of daily life. I am more reliant on my faith and spiritual practices. Every morning when I begin chemo, I say a prayer and light a candle. Many of my friends around the country do the same thing for me at the same time. Then, in the evening, I light my candle again, turn off the television, and turn on soothing music. I say another prayer and praise God for the day. Even if it was a very bad day, I praise God that I was here to experience it and perhaps help someone else.

—JOLI SPENCIER, California

12

Serenade Your Kitties

I have kitty cats and each has its own song with its name in it. Olio's song goes to the tune of "Baby Face": "O-lee-oooh. You are the cutest little O-lee-ooohh. You are my kitty and I love you so. O-leee-ohh." So, every night when I go to bed I sing their songs. They come tiptoeing in from wherever they are. Pretty soon I feel little lumps of fur snuggling in until I'm surrounded by a purring cat blanket and we all doze off into dreamland together.

—UDANA POWER, California

13

Breathe!

Relaxation breathing can calm, de-stress, focus, and relax me in several breaths. It's free and the results are immediate. No planning or equipment is required. It is such a simple thing that provides big benefits and rewards.

—VICKI L. DURY, Massachusetts

14

Keep Love Alive

On the back of our bedroom door I've created a little rogues' gallery of mug shots of friends who have died, old pals whom I still love, who look at me as knowledgeably and encouragingly as they ever did, quietly urging me to die wisely. I feel connected still—and hope somehow I am.

—BILL CLEARY, Vermont

15

Pray for Someone

Whenever I feel discouraged and think nothing could be right in my life, I try to find a quiet place to sit and write down a prayer for someone I know who needs a loving thought. Composing the words of the prayer helps align my soul with the loving Presence I need at the moment and reminds me that I am not alone in the universe—that no matter how I feel, I am truly loved and blessed.

—ELIZABETH SIMONS, Missouri

16

Slow Down

Several years ago I began the practice of deliberately slowing myself down. When I begin to feel disconnected, I walk slower, type slower, and pay close attention to my task, rather than allowing my mind to whirl around. I practice deep gratefulness during those few moments, whether it is for the green pepper I'm cutting up, the shape of the clouds outside my car window, or the smell of the tea brewing.

—LOUISE MONACELLI, Michigan

Caress the Cat

Stroking my cat several times a day has a calming and soothing effect on me. When she comes up to me, I stop whatever I'm doing to rub her silky coat and speak to her. She is my reality check when the world gets crazy, and her soft purr reminds me that I am serenely blessed.

—CAROL WILCOX, Texas

Places

God is a circle whose center is everywhere
but whose circumference is nowhere.
—ATTRIBUTED TO ST. AUGUSTINE

One day, deep in despair, I took myself to a place of great nourishment, a place I've come to call the Point of Despair. This flat piece of macadam along the river's railing is a place of healing for me. I stand there and talk to God. It is there that I surrender my despair. I trust God will take it. I continue my walk down the shore to the place I call the Point of Hope. These steps open my heart and my mind. I return to my life, cheeks glowing from the winter wind, soul soothed. This is the power of place.

18

Walk Soul to Soul with Nature

I try to find time every day to walk barefoot on the earth, even if it's just standing outside my door in the rain for a moment. I focus on the skin of my feet touching the skin of the earth—my body connecting with the body of the earth, allowing energy to flow back and forth between us. I used to think the sense of peace I experience was a gift from the earth to me, but I've heard (through the "souls" of my feet, of course!) that it's a gift we give each other—that my mindful presence and bare feet are a healing gift to the earth as her grounding presence is a gift to me.

—PATTI RIESER, North Carolina

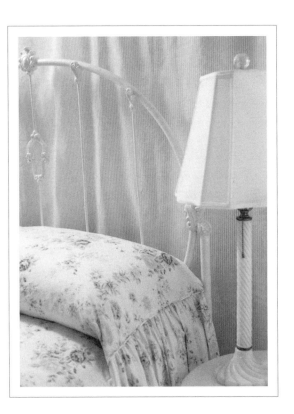

Change What You Can

When the world seems chaotic and I feel myself falling into despair and helplessness, I remember something I do control: my personal environment. So the more frightening the news, the more nurturing I make my home: The bed is made, there are no dirty dishes in the sink or clean ones on the drain board, the garbage goes out daily, clothes are hung up immediately, fragrant candles burn each evening, and so on. If I can find peace at home, it stands to reason that I can send it like a beacon of light into the world.

—REGINA LEEDS, California

20

Acknowledge Your Place in the Universe

I start my day from a *heavenly* perspective by visiting a website that posts photographs of the cosmos. Each day a different image or photograph is featured with an explanation written by a professional astronomer. When I gaze at the galaxies pictured there, at first I feel small and inconsequential. Then I begin to feel immensely privileged to be part of such a magnificent universe. My problems—really challenges and growth areas—seem manageable, and I'm eager to live my life to the fullest and to contribute something of significance to the lives of others.

—KATHLEEN HAWKINS, Texas

Plant Your Own Forest

I have planted a forest in my office! I placed a plastic sheet on the carpet and on it put three tree stumps (18" high and 15" across). Cedar chips are sprinkled all around the stumps like ground cover. On the left stump a plant resides, in the middle is a copy of the Hebrew and Christian scriptures, and on the right side is a fountain. Above the stumps is a tapestry with the phrase "Ingredients for a Happy Classroom" in the center. Around the perimeter are words and symbols highlighting those ingredients: Humor, Friendship, Kindness, Curiosity, Respect, Patience, Praise, and Recess.

—SEAN KELLY, Canada

Whistle While You Walk

As I walk down city streets or the corridors of my office building alone, I softly whistle whatever tune is in my head. It makes me happy and seems to make others smile.

—SHARRON EMMONS, Connecticut

23

Practice Gratitude

Every night before retiring, I step outside on my back patio, reach up to the sky, and thank God and the universe for this day and this life. I also keep a gratitude journal and write down at least five things I am grateful for at the end of each day.

—KAREN EVANS, Ohio

Follow Sage Advice

Something I heard from an old Dakota Sioux holy man: Take a moment to relax after a busy day. Find a nice quiet place, close your eyes, and imagine a warm white light of God shining on you from the heavens. That will chase all negative thoughts and replace them with comfort, peace, and joy.

—J.C. PRATT, Canada

25

Welcome the Day

Each morning before I dive into the hectic activities at work, I stop at a particularly beautiful place high up on the red rocks surrounding my town. I breathe in and out deliberately and consciously, aware of my connection to the Great Spirit, the true reality in all life, and within me. Sometimes I say a more formal prayer. Sometimes I shout joyously for a new day of life—a day that is like no other day before it or to come. I do what feels right for me that day. Then I come down from the mountain and go to work.

—JEROME THAILING, Arizona

26

Listen for God's Whisper

Last year I was runner-up for a national contest on the world's busiest family. Every morning, though, I rise earlier than the others, make a cup of my favorite tea, light my candle, sit in front of the window that looks out over the pond and gardens, and write down questions or thoughts that may be troubling me. I listen quietly for the answers and write them as well. It is in the stillness of daybreak that I feel God whispers to each of us.

—SUE HOLLIHAN, Canada

27

Share Your Garden

Three years ago my husband and I purchased a
vacant lot and I planted it in the pattern of the Chartres
labyrinth (a walking meditation tool). Surprisingly, my
nourishment from this project came not in the form of
walking the path myself, but in sharing it with others.

—CHRISTINE WOLF, Hawaii

28

Let the Water Heal You

Swimming. The fluidity of my body merging with the water and the meditative motion of each stroke connect me with the Divine. In the summer, I swim in the ocean. I am then reminded of being part of something so vast and unknown yet feeling so much a part of the universe, as if I really matter in that space.

—CELIA GRAND, Maine

29

Plant a Sunrise

When I moved away from the water, I missed watching the sunrise behind Mt. Rainier and the sunset behind the Olympics across Puget Sound. I needed a new way to refresh my spirit daily with nature's blessings, so I started a patio garden with a San Diego hibiscus that has new blossoms every day. First thing in the morning I look at my *sunrise* of fresh flowers to start the day.

—MELISSA JOHNSTONE ALLINGER, California

30

Stop. Look. Listen.

As a full-time working mother of two children under five, my soul-nourishing moments are captured in quick-as-sound-bite opportunities. I make it a practice to stop and absorb the beauty God provides in such abundance: the crisp air of a new fall day, a band of swans twittering as they swarm above the trees, warm sun embracing cool skin, squirrels bickering over a corncob, the stars and planets on a clear, bright night.

—LAURA ERICKSON, North Dakota

31

Go Treasure Hunting

When my husband was diagnosed with a rare form of cancer, I was devastated. My morning walks became a litany of self-pity and fear. One morning I discovered a small blue flower peeking up from behind a rock. It was simple in its beauty. I found myself smiling. Now every morning, I go treasure hunting. I always find something to inspire me: a puffy cloud, a smiling face, the color of the trees, a scurrying squirrel. Nothing out of the ordinary, yet God's handiwork. Miraculously, amid pain one can find some modicum of peace.

—CELIA L. MARSZAL, New York

32

Sense the Love
That Surrounds You

When I awaken in the early morning to the scent of my wife, the sounds of the birds, and the hush of the leaves in the trees, I am reminded how love from within me and from outside me guides me to a place of peace.

—BEN FOWLER, Maine

Things

All the things of the universe are perfect miracles,
each as profound as any.
—WALT WHITMAN

I have a fat rubber Pokémon character on my key ring. I don't know his name, but he glows in the dark. He arrived in a care package from my friend Stephen's brother, Ronnie. Ronnie lives in Kentucky and we've met only once—at Stephen's funeral in 1995. Since then, a carton from Ronnie and his family arrives at my house each year on Stephen's birthday. The box always contains a note and flavored tea, soup, and other comfort foods. One year the Pokémon guy was in there, too. This seemingly unattractive thing has come to symbolize the friendship and deep connection that was born as we shared the almost unbearable pain of losing Stephen. Each time I spot this gray and yellow creature on my key ring, it reminds me that although I am powerless over so much in life, I am always surrounded by the Creator's love. We all are.

33

Live in Rhythm

Once a week I meet with friends to drum, which loosens up all sorts of insights for all of us. I go to a conventional church in our rural area but consider Tuesday-morning drumming to be my real church. It is one time during the week when I can believe I live in a sane world.

—LAURIE PETERSEN, New York

34

Share Your Abundance

When I'm feeling disconnected from myself, I gravitate to the kitchen. Comparing inspiring recipes to available ingredients gets me back in touch, and I begin to hum old hymns as the cooking process begins. I make lots of two or three different dishes, enough for my family and a few neighbors who may be more stressed out than I am. Then I call and say I'll deliver or they can pick up something hot and savory in time for dinner. Amen! We're cookin'!

—COLLEEN MYERS

35

Create Your Own Prayer Book

I use a black-paper spiral notebook and cut out pictures from nature magazines of peaceful scenes to create my own inspirational prayer book. When I come across a wonderful quotation or a prayer I like, I copy it into my book with silver, gold, or milky-gel colored pens and paste a nature scene across from it. Just leafing through my personal prayer book calms me and gives me courage to face my day.

—R. JANE WILLIAMS, Pennsylvania

36

Maintain the Sweet Balance

Eat M&Ms! I could eat the whole bag, but to contain my consumption and nourish my soul I keep them in a box that says *M&M* and take only a few to remind me of Martha and Mary. I need to balance Mary's contemplation with Martha's action, so the balance is sweet without excess in either direction—or in chocolate.

—SHEILA OTTO, Ohio

37

Live in the Middle

I carry two little strips of paper, one in my left pocket and one in my right. My rabbi gave them to me around the time of Yom Kippur. On one is written, "For my sake was the universe created," on the other, "I am but dust." Somehow I manage to stay in the middle.

—GALE MALESKEY

Sing Out!

After my mother died, I needed to clear out her closet. What got me through was the repetition of a hymn I sang. I am no singer, but those words had deep meaning for me at that time and whenever I hear it or read the passage in the Bible, memories flood back of how good God is.

—KAREN KNEEDLER, California

Reading What Matters

I choose my reading carefully. I choose what will open my heart and open my mind—developments in science, the spirituality of many religions, health, nature, and philosophy. I read poetry, essays, and stories that open my eyes to wisdom and experience. If I can read on a garden bench in good weather or with a cup of tea beside a wide window in winter, then my soul is nourished indeed.

—BOBBIE SILK, Illinois

Create a Work of Beauty

I have recently begun providing fresh-flower arrangements for the reception area at my workplace. The weekly ritual of choosing the vessel, shopping for flowers, and slowly and mindfully creating a work of beauty has become an integral part of my soul nourishment. It provides an outlet for my creativity, centers me, and is something I really look forward to.

—JILL SHEELER-SHENK, California

Let Spirit Rock You to Sleep

Since I've passed fifty, I often wake up in the middle of the night. Instead of tossing about while chewing guilty thoughts or solving other people's problems, I now get up and move to the living room, where I read and reflect on one or two pages of a spiritual reading. This replaces the daytime meditation I've never been able to do and sends me back to sleep with a peaceful mind. Our cat usually joins me.

—RICHARD LALONDE, Canada

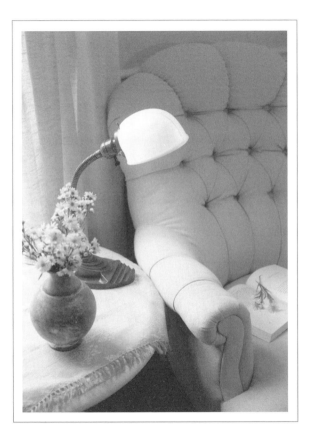

42

List What Sustains You

When I was going through a difficult separation from my husband, a friend asked me, "How do you do it?" I wrote out all the things that keep me positive and focused on what matters most: the essential role of God in my life; my gratitude for life itself; my unconditional and immeasurable love for my daughter and thankfulness for her returned love; my comfort in simply knowing my father lives; thanks for the companionship of a few good friends whom I truly care about and whose lives are an eternal fascination for me; the belief that difficulties in life are challenges that can be understood and, once understood, go away; and finally, trust in the basic goodness of humankind. I put the list on my refrigerator as a daily reminder of these irreplaceable supports.

—SUSAN THOMPSON-HOFFMAN, Maryland

43

Give Thanks for Your Bills

Instead of dreading paying my bills, I am grateful for all that those bills represent. As I write each check, I give thanks out loud for such blessings as electricity, heat, water, my mortgage, gasoline for the car, and so on. I bless all the workers at those companies who provide those goods and services and remember to be grateful for the money to pay those bills. Before I put them in the mail, I hold the envelopes in my hand one final time and send love and light out with them.

—LESLIE HOY, Pennsylvania

44

Look in the Eyes of Love

A friend designed and gave me a beautiful framed mirror only big enough for me to see my eyes. Each morning before I dress I look in the mirror and say an affirmation for the day, and every time I pass a window or mirror I meditate on the affirmation and know that God loves me.

—TONI HILL, Pennsylvania

45

Surrender Your Time

Friday is my Sabbath time of recreation. Slowly winding our pendulum clock on this day is one way I honor the sacred in ordinary time. My clock-winding prayer is the Psalm line, "My time is in your hands, O God."

—ROY HOWARD, Maryland

Pocket a Daily Spirit Word

Over a couple of years, I have collected small, smooth river rocks the size of large marbles. I have written positive yet reflective words on each one, such as love, laugh, compassion, delight, and so on. I keep these rocks in a small velvet bag. Each morning I draw one out and put it in my pocket where my hand finds it often. It becomes my daily spirit word with which I can bless myself and pass the blessing on to other souls without them even being aware.

P.S. These make a great gift for a soul friend.

—MARY THERESE BREUNING, Washington

47

Carry a Reminder

I have a small rock imprinted with the seven-circuit labyrinth (a walking meditation tool). On days when I need a boost, I carry it in my pocket to remind me that life's path is often circular, and the center of my being remains whether I am near to it or more on the fringe.

—PEGGY BABCOCK

48

Light a Family Candle

Last year for the holidays, my wife and I packed a box with special foods, one gift for each person, a tape of our favorite holiday music, and a candle with a cranberry-orange-cinnamon scent. We sent the box to my family in Florida with instructions to light the candle as they enjoyed the contents. We lit a similar candle as we opened their gifts to us. Each day now at mealtimes, we light the family candle and include our family in our prayers.

—CHUCK GOODMAN, California

Feast on Soul Food

I spent years trying to feel better by using food. I have learned, instead of overeating, to feed my soul. I've created a CD of my favorite feel-good music to listen to when my spirit is in need. Taking a walk by the lake or in the woods fills me up. So does working in my garden or giving someone I love a phone call or e-mail. By the way, I have lost over 40 pounds and kept it off for two years!

—TERI WIEST

50

Begin Again

One of my favorite quotes is from Ivy Baker Priest: "The world is round and the place which may seem like the end may also be the beginning."

Whether you choose to feed your soul by re-reading this volume from the beginning or by pursuing your own practices, may this book be the source of many fruitful beginnings for us all. Many blessings.

—ROSEMARY CUNNINGHAM, New York

To Our Readers

Red Wheel, an imprint of Red Wheel/Weiser, publishes books on topics ranging from spunky self-help, spirituality, personal growth, and relationships to women's issues and social issues. Our mission is to publish quality books that will make a difference in people's lives—how we feel about ourselves and how we relate to one another and to the world at large. We value integrity, compassion, and receptivity, both in the books we publish and in the way we do business.

Our readers are our most important resource, and we value your input, suggestions, and ideas about what you would like to see published. Please feel free to contact us, to request our latest book catalog, or to be added to our mailing list.

Red Wheel/Weiser, LLC
P.O. Box 612
York Beach, ME 03910-0612
www.redwheelweiser.com

About Spirituality & Health

Spirituality & Health magazine brings you the people, the ideas, and the practices of the current spiritual renaissance. Published six times a year, it is available in many bookstores and other newsstands or by subscription (for information call 1-800-876-8202). The companion website, *www.SpiritualityHealth.com,* offers interactive self-tests, articles, and constantly updated reviews of books, movies, audiotapes and CDs. *Fifty Ways to Feed Your Soul* is the first *Spirituality & Health* book published by Red Wheel.